Stuart Copans Thomas Singer

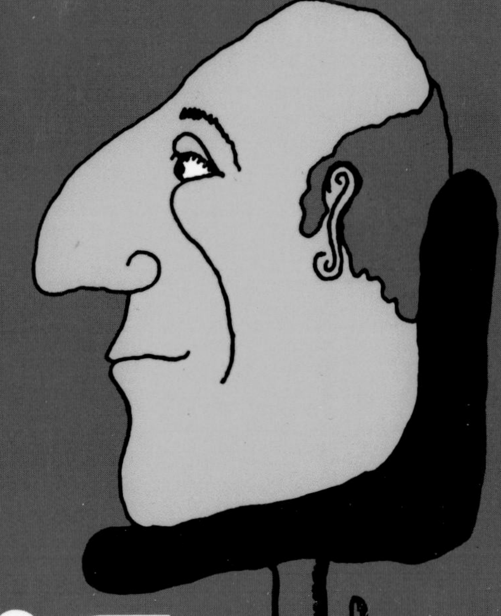

WHO'S THE PATIENT HERE?

Portraits of the Young Psychotherapist

WHO'S THE PATIENT HERE?

It appears to me, Mr. Rubin, that it's all in your head.

Who's the Patient Here?

PORTRAITS OF THE YOUNG PSYCHOTHERAPIST

STUART COPANS THOMAS SINGER

OXFORD UNIVERSITY PRESS
Oxford London New York
1978

First published as an Oxford University Press paperback, New York, 1978

Library of Congress Cataloging in Publication Data
Copans, Stu.
Who's the Patient Here?
1. Psychotherapy—Study and teaching—
Caricatures and cartoons. I. Singer, Thomas,
1942- joint author. II. Title.
RC336.C66 616.8'914'0207 78-1990 ISBN 0-19-502386-2

Printed in the United States of America

To our parents

ACKNOWLEDGMENTS

We wish to express our deep gratitude to the many patients, colleagues, and teachers who have suffered through and contributed to the creation of *Who's the Patient Here.* Among those who have touched and guided us most lovingly we are especially indebted to Gary Tucker, Ray Sobel, Steve Weissman, Roger Shapiro, Gerry Fountain, Sam Goodman, Richard Gerber, Hugh MacNamee, Malcolm Diamond, Margit Frank, Ken Keniston, Elizabeth Gay, Syd and Emly Klaus, Steve Hill, Justin Frank, John Perry, Bernie Bergen, and R. V. Glover.

We also wish to thank Nancy Dulac, Carroll Mansell, Georgia-Lee Agallianos, Sallie May, and Ilse Holan for their typing and for their patience with our many revisions of the manuscript.

CONTENTS

WHO'S THE PATIENT HERE?

PHASE I

EXPLORATION

There are probably as many reasons for choosing to become a psychotherapist as there are therapists. You may feel as though you are the first to undertake this journey: although others have taken similar paths before, yours will be new. A sense of excitement and potential discovery will help you face your early, anxious encounters with people in emotional conflict. Not unlike early explorers of new lands, you will find yourself in mysterious territory, on the edge of the known social, psychological, and biochemical world. The study of psychotherapy is a modern frontier of knowledge and human experience.

ye olde
Therapy
INSTITUTE

Psychiatry is unlike regular medicine. If in medicine the urge is to understand the machinery of the organism, in psychiatry or psychotherapy it is to gain a deep knowledge of human nature and behavior. In many ways, the attraction of psychotherapy and the preliminary momentum of engagement come from this modern search for wisdom in which your person-ness is as important as your technical information. There is the promise of a sustained, nontechnical relationship in which your learning and the patient's treatment go hand in hand.

Hello, I'm Doctor Farther! You must be the new Trainees!
RM.MD
SAC

In a secularized, technological culture, psychotherapy remains a more or less sanctioned arena in which you will be allowed to explore soulful things and yet retain membership in the established community. Here is a place where you are permitted to encounter parts of the self that are hidden, buried, unknown, or otherwise inaccessible in daily life. Through contact with the neurotic and psychotic experience, aspects of the self that are locked out of everyday reality will be open to the exploring therapist.

You've been assigned to team 2. Let me introduce you to the patients and the staff you'll be working with.
SAC

PHASE II

ANXIETY

If you come marching into your training with a sense of excitement, discovery, and the eagerness of a young Freud or Jung, you will soon meet the first obstacle—the patient. It will not be long before you find yourself secretly musing, "If it weren't for the patients, psychotherapy would be fun and fascinating."

Yet this experience of meeting patients may hold for you the initial thrill of Hiram Bingham's search for Machu Picchu. Bingham hacked his way through exotic tropical foliage along the winding Urubamba River, ever mindful of the yet undiscovered mountain center of an ancient and noble civilization. Initially, you, too, may expect to wander through a labyrinth of bizarre symptoms, thoughts and fantasies, hoping to discover the solid and healthy core of an entangled soul.

Instead, you will often stumble into the less ennobling regions of fear, suspicion, rage, doubt, and unsatisfiable longing. These potent and still undifferentiated emotions will make themselves known in a growing, perhaps gnawing discomfort which each new therapist experiences in his own way. It may be the sensation that something is sneaking up from behind and when you turn around to look, you suddenly discover that it is your own feeling of being ensnared by the heavy undergrowth.

The entanglements are thorny. Families, lawyers, employers, supervisors, nurses, and a sometimes Felliniesque cast of characters start making contradictory requests and demands. These entreaties are equaled in their intensity by the surfacing emotional conflicts of the patients, who are often as ignorant of what's happening to them as you are.

You are in a paradoxical position at best. At the very moment when you are invested with tremendous authority by patients, you may find your inner source of authority and confidence at its lowest since you began kindergarten. The dilemma of the toppling pedestal is well portrayed in the model of transactional analysis. By your patients you are seen as the bad, rejecting parent for frustrating their more regressive and demanding traits. By yourself and in projection (if not in reality) by your supervisor and institution, you are seen as the vulnerable, naughty, cowering child for feeling overwhelmed, without authority, and incompetent. Behind these two devalued images of yourself may lurk a hidden, compensatory third—the heroic and compassionate healer. Within this cherished image, you may see yourself as a therapeutic Cinderella, unappreciated and abused by your cruel stepmother supervisors, who demand that you occupy yourself with menial tasks, and "put down" by insensitive stepsister colleagues, who fail to perceive your true worth.

Let Me Out of here! I'M The Doctor!!!

At some point, you will fall. The temple of your professional identity will crumble. You will feel that there is no difference between you and your patients. Your well-developed sense of sanity will vanish and you will experience the swallowing suction of the underground. The carefully manicured sense of yourself as healer and the patient as wounded will give way. At times, you will find yourself acting and feeling as crazy as your patients. The form and content of your identification with patients will vary. Your unconscious rumblings may take a concrete form, such as forgetting a particularly difficult patient's appointment. Or you may find yourself wondering about a plot to alter the world's climate. Whatever your personal brand may be, the feeling is terrifying, and you will inwardly scream for release. It is at this critical juncture of intensified anxiety that the enormously important dialectic with your supervisor and institution with hope begins.

PHASE III
DEFENSES

Your feeling of intense anxiety and undifferentiated emotion will not last for long. A host of collective and individual defenses will be quickly marshalled to ward off the intrusion of these most unpleasant and unsettling intimations of a murky, subterranean domain.

Assuming that the discussion of deep personal trouble is anxiety-provoking for you as well as the patient, it is helpful to examine the mutually acceptable, evasive maneuvers you both use to avoid painful topics. The defenses of patients are well known and well described in the literature of psychotherapy. What are less well described are the defenses used by therapists, supervisors, and institutions. These defenses seem to develop routinely as the energy of exploration of the earliest phase is converted into the energy of avoidance. In the exciting journey of discovery you are soon assailed by an urgent desire to escape the dangers, a need to protect yourself, a yearning to go home and hide under the covers.

In many situations defenses are useful. At times they may be all we have to protect us from overwhelming anxiety and intolerable emotional pain. Furthermore, it is often a subtle and difficult process to tease out the validity of a thought or action that may be used as a defense. There is, after all, a nondefensive component to the maneuvers you will learn. There are also differences from one supervisor and institution to another in the defensive styles they support and encourage. Most training programs have institutionalized defense mechanisms, just as most therapists have individualized defense mechanisms.

Your task now is to bring these individual and institutional defenses, which are already being carried out on an unconscious basis, into awareness and to strengthen your ability to tolerate anxiety. In time, this will enable you to pay closer attention to the patient's defenses and concerns. An anatomy of the maneuvers you may find yourself using follows.

No Time now
Mr. Smith, I'll try
To see you at 3-
SAC

A. *How To Avoid Seeing the Patient*

There is a variety of techniques to ensure that the time you spend with a difficult patient is kept to an absolute minimum.

1. *"Being busy"* as a general presentation of self is an excellent tactic for keeping patients, nurses, and secretaries at a distance. "The therapist is busy" makes everyone feel guilty for placing additional demands on the overworked healer. It may also make the patient angry and this contributes to your becoming busier.

I realize I've only seen you for fifteen minutes in the last two weeks, mrs. witherspoon, but I've spent several hours with your chart.
SAC

2. The *chart* has become an increasingly important device not only for recording careful observations and collecting fees from insurance companies, but also for establishing immunity from malpractice suits and critical supervisors. More and more the chart is receiving expert and devoted medical care. It has the added advantage of safeguarding you from the patient: if the chart is properly tended, it cuts down on the time available to the patient.

3. *Meetings* are a sanctioned way of sharing information and avoiding work. Like the chart, the meeting gives you and others the feeling that your time is being used in a meaningful way and reduces the sense of guilt you may feel when not actually talking to patients. The meeting has become a more integral part of life with the rising tide of democratization, community involvement, and team planning. You can join your colleagues in relating feelings, anecdotes, and theories, with the additional advantage of getting away from patients.

This is Just to make Sure none of your crazy thoughts get out.

B. *How To Avoid Being with the Patient*

After the first line of defenses has been exhausted and you hesitantly find yourself face to face with a difficult patient, you will develop additional anxiety-reducing maneuvers for interviewing the patient without being with him or her.

1. Particularly useful with psychotic eruptions and quickly extended to any troublesome thoughts or feelings expressed by patients is the art of *"reality testing"*—focusing on their ability to recognize and integrate the multiple signals, needs, and demands of their immediate environment. In the name of these everyday concerns and preoccupations, the endangered ego of the patient will find you an eager ally. Along with your sometimes all too willing supervisor, you may hasten to "seal over" the crazy talk with intense social manipulation through the magical use of words like "APPROPRIATE." This is a highly effective tool in helping fragile patients cope with terrifying images or emotions and in satisfying your need to structure, comprehend, and control. As a defense, "reality testing" can be used to deny the meaning and potential value of unconscious fantasies.

You are a lovely laurel Tree, Miss Daphne.

2. *Going along with the patient's craziness* can be developed into a most intriguing defensive style. By encouraging the profuse production of personal mythologies, you can avoid connecting these fascinating fantasies to their source in the patient's anxiety and need for change. The detailed exploration of the patient's inner world allows you to feel tolerant and open-minded. It provides plentiful material for professional exchange and protects you from the pain of engaging the anguished patient.

Now Just speak into The micvophone, mvs. Jones
Now Just speak into The microphone mrs. Jones

3. Advanced *technological gadgetry* can be skillfully introduced to distract and bedazzle therapist and patient alike. The lure of recorded recognition, instant replay, and fantasied stardom nourishes the illusion of creating something real and forever. Furthermore, the recording instruments can serve as a protective barrier to separate you from the patient.

This Pill should help you feel better, mr. Smith.

4. Focusing primarily on *medication* is one of the time-honored ways of confining the discussion to areas where you and the patient are comfortable. You can enjoy the feeling that something is being done, something given, while you preserve a mutually acceptable distance. Should conversation lull, side effects, dosage, and schedules provide excellent diversions, which are almost as safe and neutral as the weather.

It appears to me, Mr. Rubin, that it's all in your head.

5. As you begin to develop confidence and skill, your techniques for avoiding being with patients while talking with them will become more subtle and sophisticated. Viewing the patient as a *metapsychological construct* is an invaluable way of gaining control of yourself and the patient.

A multitude of theories will permit you to reduce and codify the complexity of human experience. Wtih a psychological bias, all body can be seen as psyche, and from a biological bias, all psyche becomes body. Either view lets you perpetuate the mind/body split.

SAC

SUPEREGO
EGO
ID

These models can become highly refined maneuvers that will help you substitute cardboard representations for human reality. They take many forms, depending on the institutional focus:

a. If the institution is analytically oriented, you can view the patient as a psychodynamic formulation.

DMS
III
Diagnos
MANUAL
DIAGNOSTIC MANUAL
291.1 or
291.3 or even
291.9 or 292.1
292.9 or 293.0 Chair
or 293.2 or Chair
293.4 or 293.5 Chair
or 294.1
or 294.3 Chair
or 294.8 Chair
or 295.2
or 295.3 Chair
or 295.4 or 296.0 or 296.1
or 295.6 or 296.2 or 296.3
or 295.7 or 296.8 or 297.0 Chair
or 295.90 or 297.1 or 297.9
or 300.6 or
301.2 or 301.3 or 301.5 Chair
or 302.4 or 303.2
or 303.9
or 304.7 CHAIR
or 304.5
or 307.3
or 308.4 or
308.9 or 319.2

b. If the institution specializes in evaluation, you can safely view the patient as a diagnostic category.

CH_3
CH_3
CH_3
SAC

c. If the institution favors the biochemistry of mental illness, the patient may tend to appear as an aberrant molecule.

Actually Mr. Jones, you're
not depressed. You've just
developed a maladaptive
response repertoire as a
result of a series of
inadvertant stimulus-
response contingencies.
SAC

d. If the institution is concerned with social acceptability and adaptability, you can look at the patient as a piece of behavior in need of modification.

I think I've discovered the problem in your family. Little Herbie is the family scapegoat.
HERBIE

e. If group and family therapy models prevail they may be as exciting as your first erector set. They provide endless possibilities for mapping complex configurations and currents of behavior, emotions, and roles.

you Leo's are all alike, Mr. Jones,
your Kundalini is stuck in the second chakra.

f. If the institution gravitates toward the countercultural edge of the new age and its emerging therapies, you can intuit the patient's astrological disharmony and its need for karmic re-location.

Just relax ms. ANDRogeny— we need to take a brain Scan of your AURA.

g. If you follow the new breed of biological mystics who have wed futuristic technology and ancient esoteric wisdom, you can become a biofeedback guru and choose from an enticing array of techniques. This movement's marriage of science and religion, body and spirit, may seem like a grown-up Disneyland to you—childish, fantastic, and alluring.

We're pretty fluid here — You can either leave Cerebus here for his session, or you can stay and participate in his therapy.
ARF INC.
ARF INC.
SOUTHERN MARIN
AUTHORIZED
DOG ROLFING
AND
REBIRTH CENTER
Specializing in AFGHans

h. If you find yourself in an environment where everyone is becoming a licensed or unlicensed therapist of one kind or another, it may be difficult to know who and what is of substance and value. Burgeoning therapies and their practitioners may leave you scratching your head in bewildered disbelief or waving your arms in outraged protest.

SAC

6. Should medication, reality testing, technology, and metapsychological constructs fail to keep the patient at a safe distance during the interview, you can

a. daydream about something more pleasant or at least something outside the room;

SAC

b. see yourself as a helpless puppet who cannot function without the supervisor's guiding hand;

ZZZZZ
SAC

c. and, if all else fails, fall asleep.

No, mr. witherspoon, I won't give you a bandaid. Why don't we spend The next FIFTY minutes analyzing why you had a car accident on your way to our session. Then you can seek some medical help.

7. A defense that satisfies the patient's stereotype of the cold, indifferent analyst, as well as your need to protect yourself from the pain of empathy and your desire to be seen as a seasoned blank-wall therapist, is to religiously avoid giving support to the patient.

SAC

8. Conversely, perhaps the most elegant and enduring defense of all for the young therapist is to be consistently, persistently, and thoroughly nice and supportive. There is almost no way for either you or the patient to break through this formidable barrier. Your need to be nice and to be liked can keep both of you in a lukewarm broth which can last indefinitely.

I do understand Barb. I have exactly the same problem with my lover.

9. In an era of first name informality, you can carry the role of being nice and supportive even further and develop it into a full-blown pseudointimacy. Not only does this feel good for a while, but used defensively it permits you to escape your task as a therapist by being self-revealing.

AND TODAY-HA!-HA!-
SHE THREATENED TO
BLOW ME UP!
HB
HB
TNT

C. *How To Undo Being with the Patient*

There are many ways of decompressing at the end of an interview or course of therapy. Two prominent methods are cynicism and humor, and they are especially useful in case presentations, team meetings, and peer interactions.

After a particularly intense session, forced humor may help you ward off the impact of a threatening experience.

And then
she said "I wish I were dead. I'm going to
Jump in The ToileT!!!

Cynicism will occasionally help protect you from the pathos, loneliness, despair, and sadness that you will encounter.

D. *How To Get Rid of the Patient*

Getting rid of the patient after a single session, a brief hospitalization, or a prolonged course of psychotherapy is perhaps the most refined and difficult of the defensive arts.

Medical doctors sometimes use the phrase "dumping a turkey" to describe getting rid of a bad patient. In modern psychotherapeutic practice, there is a more elaborate (and disguised) vocabulary for the same activity. The goal of the process, whatever its label, is divesting oneself of exhausting, infuriating, or otherwise demoralizing patients. One of your more satisfying therapeutic triumphs may be to find a medical cause for a psychiatric symptom that will permit you to transfer the patient to another specialty service.

Not quite, Mr. charbel.
This week we meet at 2:00 PM Tuesday
and 4:15 PM wednesday. Last week we met at 1:45 PM
Monday and 3:15 PM Thursday, and next week we will
meet at
10:15 AM Monday
and 11:00AM
Friday.

Other ways of getting rid of the patients are

1. to schedule the patients at odd times and vary the time each week;
2. to avoid following up on patients who miss appointments;
3. to provoke patients into quitting by being late, interrupting sessions with phone calls, and adopting other tactics to annoy and withdraw from them.

It seems clear, Mr. Reshick, that you have some deep-seated Problems that make it impossible for you to succeed in a responsible position. unfortunately you need a responsible position To afford my Therapy.

Should these fail, you can

1. decide the patient isn't ready to commit himself to *real* therapy;
2. adjust the clinic's fee so that she can't afford therapy;
3. announce that you specialize in crisis intervention and that the patient has deep-seated problems requiring long-term treatment, so that he must be transferred to another agency;
4. intuit that the patient's problems require a therapist of the opposite sex from you and refer the patient to someone else;
5. determine that the patient has received maximum benefit from what you have to offer and that continued therapy would be unproductive or might even lead to regression.

Actually, Mr. Linden, although you may not realize it yet, You are all better.

When these tactics don't work, you can tell the patient he or she is cured.

But you can't stop yet Mrs. Holland. you're still not perfect.

Holding on to the patient in the relentless pursuit of insight appears to be the opposite of getting rid of the patient. What you get rid of is the pain of separating and letting go. You eliminate the difficult work of examining your need of the patient, the patient's need of you, and the limitations of patients, therapists, and therapy.

I agree Mrs. Laurel-
perhaps our therapy
would go better if
I weren't so closely
Tied to this institution.

A final, potent defense involves projection and rage against the institution, which is seen as presenting limits and responsibilities that make good therapy impossible. Although partly grounded in reality, this paranoid stance allows you to avoid facing your own anxieties and personal limitations by projecting your internal conflicts onto a supervisor, training director, department, hospital, or any of a variety of governmental agencies.

Scapegoating other therapists and organizations can be done in collusion with your patient. This deflects the patient's frustration, dissatisfaction, and anger with you as a therapist and with the failure of your treatment. Both of you can pretend that it is someone else's fault and that neither of you is responsible for the mess.

When your own feelings of anger, frustration, and impotence are made known to the *system,* institutional authorities may respond to you with hostile interpretations, leading to further polarization and isolation. The final outcome of this defensive impasse may be the conviction that the institution is bad, and that if only you could meet outside the precinct of its evil influence a real and meaningful process could unfold.

Yes, Dr. SCHWAB is in his last year of Training; however he is still seeing selected new patients. leave your number and I'll have him call you.
Dr. W.H. SCHWAB

Just as you may rage against the institution, you will also depend on it for protection and nurturance. You will protect yourself by invoking its rules and regulations. For instance, the institutional shield permits you to send away bothersome patients if they live in another catchment area. Institutional nurturance and your dependence on it will be everywhere—from your desk and secretary to your peers, teachers, and patients. You will need this support more than you wish to acknowledge.

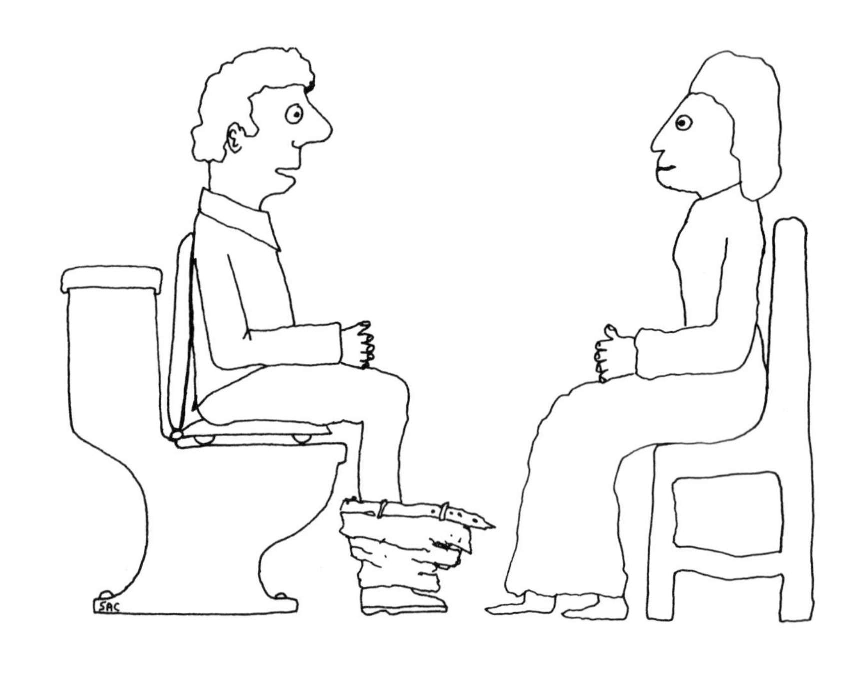
SAC

PHASE IV

FEARS AND WISHES

As your initial anxiety subsides and your defenses ease, a different kind of anxiety, less diffuse and undifferentiated, develops. It is directly related to the ongoing reciprocal relationship between you and an individual patient. This anxiety is most easily described in terms of the underlying feelings, the fears and wishes, activated by the relationship.

These processes are difficult to categorize. They are not fixed patterns, but are rather shifting configurations in which what is a wish at one moment can become a fear or defense the next. What is experienced at one moment as your fear and the patient's wish, may in the next instant become your wish and the patient's fear.

These images and feeling-states do not exist either in the sealed container of the patient's psyche or in the insulated chamber of your mind. They grow out of the interactive field between you and the patient. Some of the images most often associated with fear and anger on the part of the therapist follow.

Most beginning therapists fear exposure. It is natural for you to fear that patients, peers, and supervisors will see and focus on your human imperfections. At times, you may wish and need to expose yourself.

1

2
Kleenex

In the fear of exposure you may present supervisors with ambiguous and distorted accounts of your interactions with patients. This skewing of material serves to temporarily maintain your self-esteem and to please your teachers, whose approval and validation of you as a skillful, sensitive person will seem most important. The thought of their mocking judgment can be devastating, and at times you will do anything to avoid feeling incompetent and ignorant.

EXTRA! EXTRA! READ ALL ABOUT IT!
EXTRA!
SHRINK
ACCUSED

You may fear scandal or wish for notoriety.

AND HOW ARE YOU TODAY GENERAL GRANT — I MEAN MR. BEASLEY?
50
A
FIFTY
FIFTY
FIFTY DOLLARS
50

You may wonder whether treatment is worth the patient's time and money. The patient may be right in his suspicious accusations of your unconscious greed.

And yet, with some patients, no matter what they pay you, it will not be enough to cover the emotional cost to you of being with them. Money may be more difficult for you than sex, and along with your training institution you may deny its financial realities and psychological meaning in the name of altruism.

I'm in Such pain, Doctor. I can't understand why you don't help me.

You may fear inadequacy and helplessness or find solace in these feelings.

Silence may be terrifying to you and the patient. Together you may talk about anything to avoid its awkwardness and emptiness, and thus its potential value escapes you.

you know, Mr. Jones, we really can't get much work done if you insist on hanging there and saying nothing.
SAC

You will fear that patients may commit suicide and may secretly hope that they will succeed.

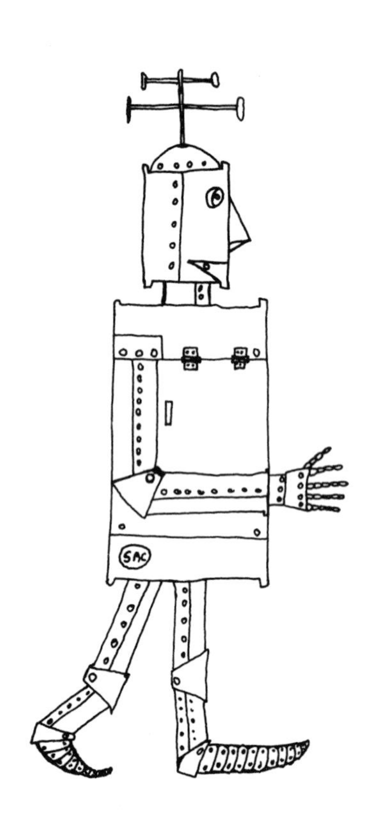
SAC

You may fear the possibility that your professional role will encroach on and eventually stifle your unique individuality. This fear of dehumanization may lead to a wish to be more personal. On the other hand, you may wish to use your professional mask to hide your personal idiosyncrasies.

YOU ARE A BASTARD, MR. JONES!!

You may fear and wish to confront painful truths about patients and yourself.

you seem angry Today, miss Ascott.

You may fear and seek expression of your patient's anger as well as your own.

I wonder why you're peeing on my couch, Mr. Smith, when there is a bathroom next to my waiting room?

In the fear of guiltily experiencing yourself as cruel, arbitrary, sadistic, and less than perfect, you may steadfastly avoid setting any limits at any time.

Before presenting this Golden Couch award to the best therapist of the year, I'd like to tell you all that not only did this person have the highest overall cure rate this year, she also had only one patient sign out against medical advice, had no complaints about her from referring physicians or agencies, kept all her records up to date, and was voted "the person I'd most like to do cotherapy with" by 83% of our staff. without further elaboration I'd like to present this award to...

Competitive and rivalrous feelings toward your colleagues (and patients) will be difficult for you and your peers. You may feel that you are all alone, out of it—that other trainees are more knowledgeable, experienced, and competent. Or you may want to be special and believe that you have an extraordinary talent.

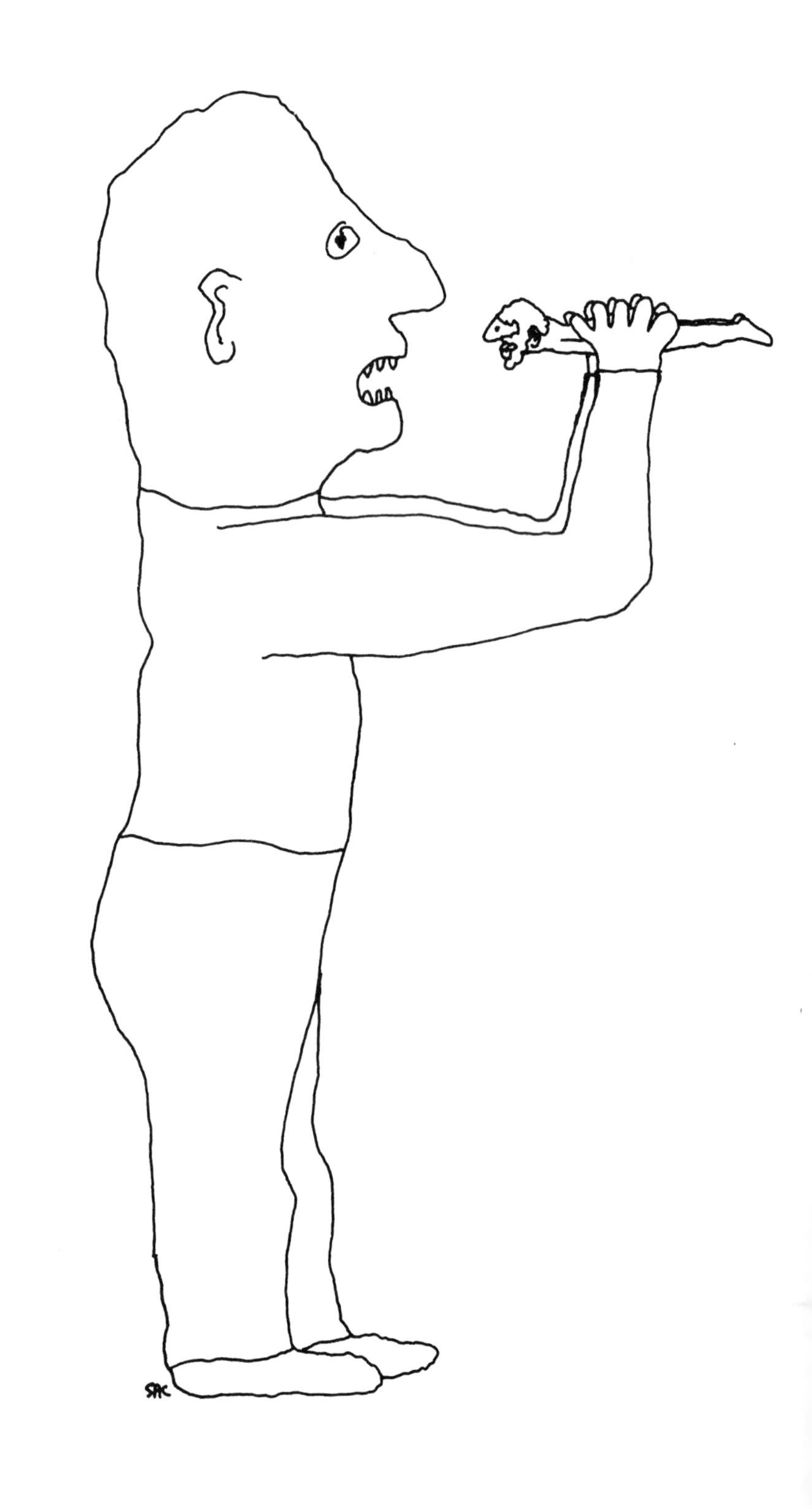

The demands, dependency, and emotional hunger of patients are sometimes voracious. Your own neediness is likely to be more disguised.

SAC

Your fear of being fooled by patients will probably be matched by your fear of being a charlatan.

AND WHAT ElSE DO YOU AND THE MilKMAN DO WHEN YOU HAVE WHAT YOU CAll KiNKY SEX MRS. LA BElly?

Your voyeuristic curiosity may embarrass you and prevent you from asking necessary questions. It may also keep you focused on only one area. The patient's curiosity about your intimate life will be even more intense and ambivalent.

Touching and being touched will frighten and attract you and your patients.

You're right, miss Affler, it's not a conventional psychiatrist's couch. After my last patient it folds out into a hide-a-bed. And my chair folds out into a combination refrigerator, hot plate, and TV.

You may wish to use relationships with patients to conceal and mitigate your own loneliness and inability to relate. Or, you may fear that intense involvement with patients will cut you off from the world outside your office.

SAC

You may be afraid that exploration of the inner life of patients
will unlock doors

SAC

behind which lurk dangerous phantoms and forces.

SAC

Once released, these fantasies will grow

and engulf you as well as the patient.

SAC

Or, alternatively, they will exhaust and annihilate you,

leaving the patient refreshed and renewed.

MR. JONES! MR. JONES! Now that we've finally broken through your resistances where are you?

At times you may fear that what lurks behind the patient's defenses is not an engaging and terrifying fantasy, but rather an awesome void. You may also fear to encounter your own inner emptiness.

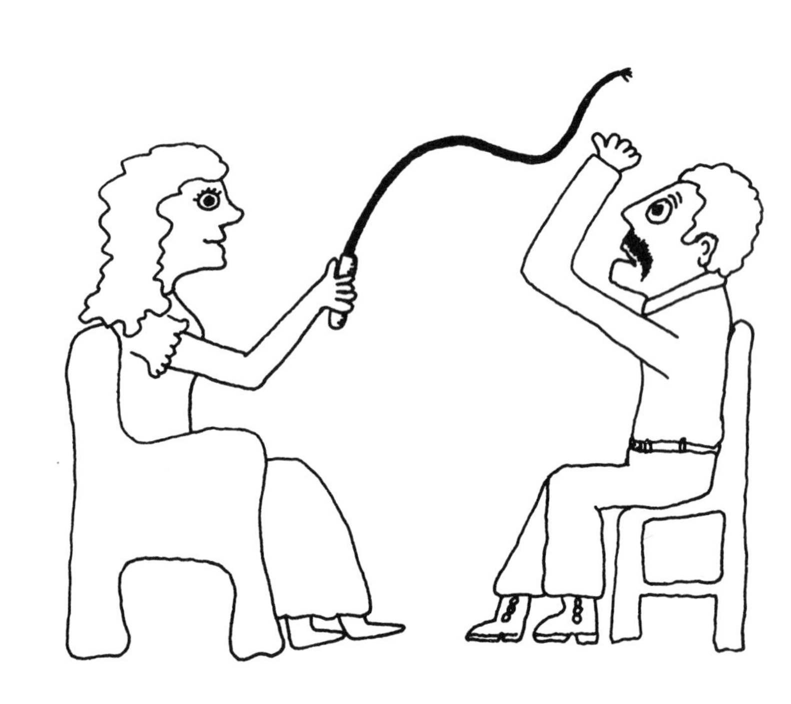

If unlocking the doors to the patient's fantasy life is threatening, even more so is the fear and wish that in the process your own crazy and unacceptable urges will be unleashed. Among these forbidden impulses which may startle and shame you are the following:

1. Your impulse to control, punish, or simply hurt the patient.

SAC

2. Your impulse to identify and merge with the patient.

SAC

3. Your wish to give birth to a new person through the creative act of therapy,

4. or through your own enlightening, transforming power.

5. Once the miraculous birth has occurred, your nurturing, maternal impulses may be a cause for discomfort and secret longing.

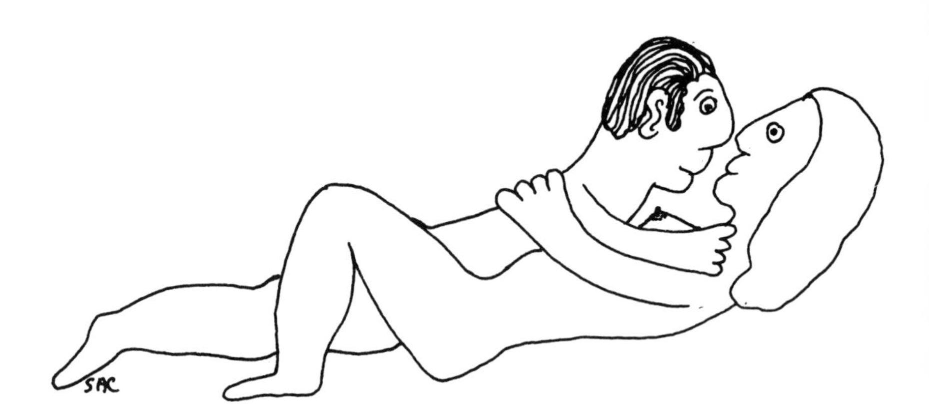
SAC

6. Your sexual impulses, both heterosexual

7. and homosexual, are officially recognized and expected, but will still be unnerving.

8. Your love and compassion for the patient will rarely be discussed.

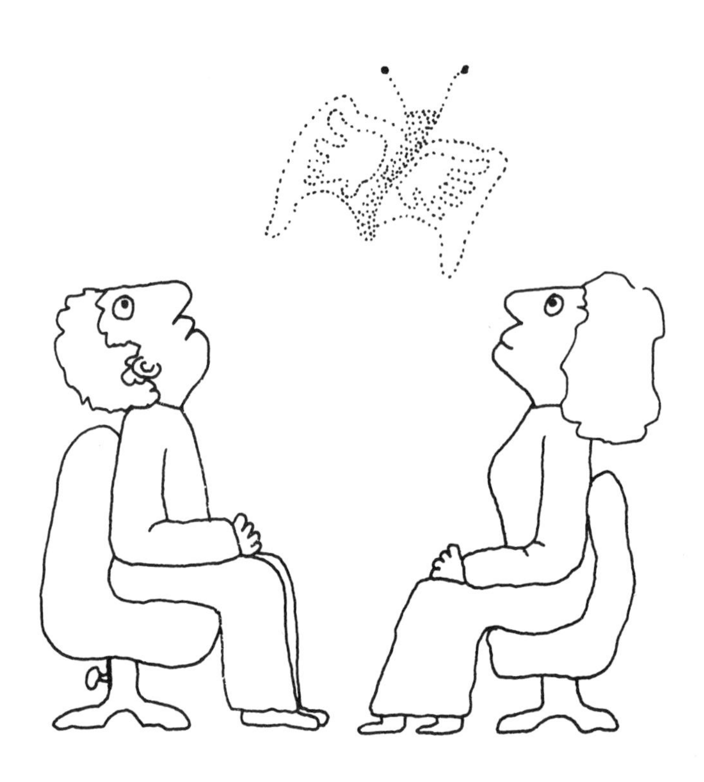

PHASE V

INTEGRATION

If, as a beginning therapist/explorer, you set off in search of a fabled city of the mind and heart, your path and goal may undergo a transformation as the journey proceeds. Whether you discover Machu Picchu or not, you may learn to see more clearly and to feel more deeply. Clarity of vision and depth of feeling are not easily attained, and in struggling to differentiate what belongs to you, to your patients, and to your institutional community you may get only fleeting glimpses of yourself as a skillful and humane therapist.

It is easy, and maybe necessary, to joke about the agonies of training and the absurdities of theories, institutions, patients, and therapists. But to grasp what makes it work, what makes it meaningful, is more difficult.

You may stumble into moments when all your training makes sense, when it comes together in an instant that transcends your personal experience and concerns. These rare moments of integration seem to touch the deeper mysteries of existence. Whether they occur within or outside the framework of an established set of theoretical doctrines is irrelevant.

You may be struggling with a difficult patient and suddenly discover that you feel deeply in tune and are able to be more compassionate and insightful. The patient may respond in kind, and you will be startled to see something emerge between you of which neither one of you is the individual creator. These moments are delicate and tender. Their very fragility may cause you to shy away from talking about them or even acknowledging that they occur. It is easier and more fitting for the heroic healer to talk about monsters than butterflies.

DENIAL
SUPER EGO
SUBLIMATION
MOTHER
PROJECTION
EGO
FATHER
ISOLATIO
ID
CHILD
HELP ME
REPRESSION
REACTION FORMATION

One of the reasons it is difficult to elucidate the process of integration is that it is cyclical. Your flashes of insight into murky experiences will fade quickly, and other dark phases of confusion and doubt will follow. A few of the elements in these brief moments of integration or illumination are worth noting.

You will witness the joy of an unexpected stride in development or breakthrough in feeling—both in patients and in yourself. You will share a communion with trusted colleagues and supervisors. In time, you may give thanks to an institution which sustains, honors, and even expands your personal strengths and at the same time tolerates and helps you accept your limitations. You may not appreciate the institutional support while in the midst of training, and yet later sense that many people were helpful in ways you never suspected or could acknowledge at the time. Leaving the institution, your strongest emotions may be of relief and anger, which will only gradually shift to affection and gratitude.

You will discover the vitality of many diverse theories. What may be hardest is not to find a good theory, but how to use and integrate many valid theories. These theories will not only save you from drowning, but also guide and enrich you.

In training, you will be surrounded by the institution and the patients. All aspects of your personal life will tend to be colored by the training program. You will come to feel that you exist only as a trainee. It is necessary to experience this immersion, but at times it will seem never-ending. You will become too closely identified with the role of therapist and may learn to retreat behind your newly acquired skills.

One goal is to grasp that personal and professional selves can nourish and yet be separate from one another. Learning that they can co-exist, not in a cold war conflict, but in active and harmonious relation to one another, is a most difficult task. You may begin to live only for psychopathology and feel that all that is justifiable or real in the world is related to your work. Or you may find yourself rigidly separating and guarding your personal life from your professional life. Isolating the two or fusing with your role as a therapist are equal hazards.

AND WHAT WOULD HAPPEN IF YOU TOLD HIM HOW YOU FEEL?

The potential for authority and responsibility residing in your professional identity can be intoxicating as well as frightening. As healer, you will seek to possess dangerous and seductive power. Derived from your deepening knowledge of the psyche, this wisdom may lead to insights that shatter unhappy, airtight lives or transform frogs into princes. You may find yourself drawing patients toward self-knowledge that can be poisonous and/or healing.

You will need to recognize your own vulnerability. Learning not to be afraid to experience your personal conflicts in the work you do with patients will be one of your hardest tasks.

As patients begin to unveil their deeper feelings of pain and joy, hate and love, hurt and tenderness, your own deep wounds may be touched and opened. Recoiling in quiet fear and defensiveness will have the likely effect of closing off the depths to which both of you may be moved. You may feel that to experience your own conflicts in therapy is unprofessional and manipulative, that you are using your patients to solve your own problems. The guilt that this evokes is real, and yet, if you respond to it with shame and withdrawal, you may deprive both yourself and the patient of an opportunity to explore and heal old wounds. The wish to cure yourself in work with patients is natural—not to be trampled or dismissed.

You will want to use your personal experience in therapy and to learn from therapy how to better conduct your own life. Professional and personal integration are parallel processes that go hand in hand. Eventually, they may become less interdependent and you may not need or use patients to undo or solve your own problems. But this gradual differentiation is attained through experiencing yourself in therapy, not by rigorously removing yourself from the process. Experiencing your own wounds in therapy does not mean that you expose them to patients. It does mean that you are open to them.

AND not only have I lost 20 pounds since you helped me understand why I was overeating, but I no longer have Fantasies of gorging myself.

As you discover in the everyday frustrations of becoming and being a therapist that you are not perfect, that you have problems, that you make mistakes, you will become less demanding of yourself and of patients. In accepting your limitations, your striving for perfection may diminish. You may even begin to see patients resolving conflicts that remain problematic for you.

Hi dear. How were Things at the clinic Today?

Often it may seem you are spending so much of your energy working on other people's problems that you do not have enough for your own. Much of what goes on in therapy will deplete you.

1. Patients will assist you in making mistakes. They will put you into difficult positions where nothing you do is right. They will enjoy your fumbling efforts to appear competent.
2. Your personal authenticity will constantly be tested by patients and society. As a result, you may look for peaceful release in pursuing mindless, mechanical tasks and hobbies.
3. Often your work will be boring, and no matter what you do, some patients will not change. They will not even have interesting fantasies.
4. There will be bad days when you are not present as an alert and sensitive guide.

you're not crazy, you're stupid!
I'm not stupid, I'm crazy!

5. You may find yourself engaged in ridiculous battles which are lively and bewildering.
6. You will make technically impeccable interpretations with excellent timing and perfect wording that go nowhere. You will also do unconscionable things that turn out to be productive.
7. Theories don't explain everything and don't necessarily work. This may be both disturbing and liberating.
8. The need for recognition and approval in an intangible and ambiguous field may make you yearn to be a carpenter, the fruits of whose labor have a visible structure.

As you discover the extent to which you, patients, theories, and institutions are limited and flawed, you will begin to discard the individual and collective defenses that have provided protection but have also narrowed the scope of your involvement with patients.

As you realize that your striving for perfection leads to systematic disillusionment and exhaustion, a new orientation and attitude will emerge—more vital, humane, and lighthearted. The anxiety, defenses, fears, and wishes were serious, often painful, and only occasionally relieved by ironic humor. There may be another kind of humor in which the playfulness, openness, and infinite variety of human experience emerge more fully.

You will work with children who rekindle your own youthfulness and sense of wonder. You will be humbled and enriched by some older patients whose age, experience, and wisdom exceed your own.

NO Mrs. SHEPHERD, THIS is NOT A THERAPEUTIC MANEUVER. It's A MISTAKE. But perhaps we can learn from it.

You will begin to see that your points of weakness and ignorance can be helpful as well as obstructive. These humiliating defects will serve as a gateway through which you and the patient come together in a more deeply human relation. Along with a growing acceptance of your vulnerability, a more grounded sense of inner authority and sensitivity will take root.

PSYCHIATRY / PSYCHOLOGY

WHO'S THE PATIENT HERE?

Written and illustrated by two psychiatrists-in-training, this book is a cartoon guide to the variety of feelings commonly experienced by beginning psychotherapists and other helping professionals, be they psychiatrists, social workers, counselors, teachers, bartenders, or cab drivers. The various defensive and evasive maneuvers trainees learn to use in order to deal with the complexities and demands of therapeutic relationships often cause them to feel guilty. They discuss these maneuvers only with great difficulty. The disillusionment of idealistic beginners can end in cynicism and despair or it can find a middle ground of informed humanism. This witty book gives a sympathetic and insightful view of their anxieties. The authors point out the commonness, necessity, and even therapeutic value of these training experiences. The book also explores the complicated relationship between institutions, supervisors, therapists, and patients and raises important questions about the training of psychotherapists. Here is a fresh and candid view that anyone entering the helping professions will appreciate and that is certain to interest anyone undergoing psychotherapy.

Stuart Copans is Director of Child and Adolescent Services at the Brattleboro Retreat. Thomas Singer is a psychiatrist in private practice.

A GALAXY BOOK
OXFORD UNIVERSITY PRESS
NEW YORK

Cover design by Egon Lauterberg

GB 545 / $5.95

ISBN 0-19-502386-2